Page 1. View up the James River from downtown
Pages 2 and 3. View to the southwest over Byrd Park
Pages 6 and 7. Capitol Square at night

Edited by John G. Zehmer

Designed by Donald G. Paulhus

Produced by Fort Church Publishers, Inc.
Little Compton, R.I. 02837

Distributed by Historic Richmond Foundation
2407 East Grace Street
Richmond, Virginia 23223

Printed in Japan

OLD RICHMOND TODAY

Photography by Richard Cheek

Introduction & Text by John G. Zehmer

Published by The Council of
Historic Richmond Foundation

Introduction

Old Richmond Today is the celebration of a communal heritage. The city belongs to all – citizen and visitor alike. To live in Richmond is a privilege; to visit is a pleasure. Richard Cheek's pictorial survey vividly confirms these observations.

The book is less a guidebook than a testament to a century of achievements in historic preservation, collected for the first time in full color in a single volume. The city's major landmarks and museums are shown along with other efforts, not only those of organizations and institutions, but also those of generations of Richmonders who have successively lived, worked and played in the city's buildings, neighborhoods and parks. Unfortunately such subjects are so numerous that all could not be included; thus sites in old Manchester, the more recently annexed suburbs and the surrounding counties await a subsequent study.

Three basic facts underlie the history and appearance of Richmond. The existence of the Falls of the James River creates a dramatic setting where the flat coastal region meets the rolling Piedmont. The establishment of the state capital here in 1780 thrust the city into its role of leadership. The selection of the city as the capital of the Confederate States of America gave Richmond a singular experience in American history which particularly fascinates many visitors, especially those who come from abroad.

The Falls rendered the city the natural site for a major trading center. This situation, in turn, led to the construction of the canals and, subsequently, to Richmond's becoming the gateway to the South for railroads and interstate highways.

The choice of Richmond as the state capital resulted in a concentration of people and a focus of ideas that have influenced both its heritage and its character. All aspects of society in the state – government, business, medicine, religion, industry, culture – have special representation in the capital city.

Richmond's role as the wartime capital of a sovereign nation from 1861 to 1865 imprinted a mystique that today is more imagined by outsiders than experienced by natives. If the Confederate era were Richmond's only claim to fame, it might be different. As a city that honors heroes of the American Revolution and still argues the relative merits of Jefferson's and Marshall's precepts of government, Richmond is able to put its tumultuous Civil War history into perspective. The appropriation of funds by a city council with a black majority to conserve the statues of Southern generals exemplifies the strides in sensitivity and understanding achieved in a city that has endured and survived epic social change.

Richmond does not have the concentrated, romantic image of Charleston or Savannah. It is a large sprawling city – urbane and picturesque, crowded and bucolic, noisy and peaceful, hallowed and profane. It was spared the worst of the urban renewal movement of the 1950s and '60s, even though it was rent by road construction and injured by several large-scale development projects. Nevertheless, much remains to serve as a brilliant counterpoint to new buildings raised over the last century.

For many years preservationists had a less than perfect working relationship with city and state administrations. In the 1970s this improved, as planners and architects were convinced that rehabilitation was an acceptable and feasible solution to modern needs. Federal tax credits became available, and preservation came of age.

The roles of city and state governments in preservation during the last quarter century cannot be overstated. In Richmond, both city and state maintain inventories of historic buildings, spaces, statues and public rights-of-way, which *in toto* surpass the holdings of many other jurisdictions combined. The state's properties include such stellar examples as the Capitol, the Science Museum and the holdings of Virginia Commonwealth University. Of equal significance are the brick sidewalks and gaslights of Church Hill, the monuments and paving blocks of Monument Avenue, and the rows and rows of trees everywhere in Richmond – all lovingly maintained by the city. Visitors invariably are impressed that there is so much to experience in Richmond.

Credit is due to the legions of public servants who have cooperated in so many ways over the years.

Beginning in the 1890s, early efforts by the Virginia Historial Society, the Valentine Museum, the Confederate Memorial Literary Society, the Association for the Preservation of Virginia Antiquities (APVA) and The Woman's Club were typical of their time in that they focused on museum-type presentations, single-building adaptations or commemorative sites. The founding of the William Byrd (Richmond) Branch of the APVA in 1935 and of its offspring, the Historic Richmond Foundation in 1956, marked the beginning of a broadened interest in neighborhoods and districts. The Branch has maintained its concern with specific projects, complementing the Foundation's general neighborhood undertakings and educational programs.

This book is neither a history nor a promotional tract. It is an attempt to draw together a visual record of buildings, artifacts and sites that have come down to us from the past – an amazingly rich legacy. The Richmond that exists today was created by thousands of individuals who built homes, founded businesses, planted flowers and placed monuments and tombstones for more than two centuries. Much is owed to those who have gone before; likewise, much should be expected of those who assume stewardship in the 21st century.

Acknowledgments

In the preparation of this book many people participated in many, varied ways. Without the support of the trustees of Historic Richmond Foundation, the idea would never have come to fruition. In accepting the challenge to raise funds and handle the costs of preparation, publication and distribution, the Council of Historic Richmond Foundation made it a reality. The joint committee of council members and HRF trustees, all of whom contributed considerable amounts of time, included Janis Carrell, Helen Reveley, Eleanor Maxwell, Judy Brown, Lynette Alley, Eve Bowman, Edward D. C. Campbell, Drew St. J. Carneal and Calder Loth. The support of Messrs. D. Tennant Bryan, J. Stewart Bryan III and James S. Evans at Media General; Mr. and Mrs. Lawrence Lewis; Mr. and Mrs. Eppa Hunton V; and Mrs. William T. Reed, Jr., is acknowledged with sincere appreciation as is that of the William Byrd Branch of the APVA. Through their generosity, these benefactors made feasible a major goal – publication at a price accessible to the general public.

We are indebted to the staffs of the public buildings and museums pictured, who came in at odd times and willingly made special arrangements for us. To list them individually would mean repeating most of the list of subjects. For special favors we owe thanks to Andrew J. Asch, Jr., James H. Whiting, Saul Viener, Reynolds Metals Company,

Lewis E. Ferguson Painting Company, John Rick and Thompson & McMullan. For the use of photographs by Richard Cheek, we are grateful to the Maymont Foundation.

For their help in setting up for photography in different locations, we thank many city employees, especially members of the Department of Public Works, Department of Public Safety, Department of Public Utilities and The Mosque. Thanks also go to old friends in the city's Department of Community Development: Richard Morse, Donald Charles, Veda Boswell and John Albers. On behalf of the Commonwealth of Virginia, Governor and Mrs. Gerald L. Baliles, Wendell Seldon, Alan Platt, Mary Jane Tayloe, the Capitol Police and the Virginia Commonwealth University Police all facilitated our work. At VCU Dr. Alastair Connell, Cheryl Yeaman and students in Gladding Residence Center made special photographic opportunities available.

In the preparation of the manuscript, I was assisted by several who helped improve and clarify my imprecise prose. Most of the committee read and made suggestions as did Anthony Binga, Dr. Francis Foster, Margaret T. Peters and Judy Anderson. Throughout the endeavor, meaningful encouragement and support was provided by Richard Cheek's parents, Mr. and Mrs. Leslie Cheek, Jr., and by our enthusiastic wives, Betsy Cheek and David Zehmer.

Without the staff at Historic Richmond Foundation this book would never have been completed. The help, counsel and good humor of Pamela B. Michael, Carole D. Haith, Melinda P. Skinner and Sarah S. Driggs are noted with deep appreciation.

Finally, it is a pleasure to salute the other three parties in our production quartet: Richard Cheek, the photographer; Donald Paulhus, the designer; and James Patrick, the publisher. That four individuals with such strong opinions could easily agree on the selection and layout of more than a hundred subjects came as a surprise to each of us. I can only surmise that Richmond itself was the muse that guided the four of us to so harmonious a conclusion. To record his native city, Richard Cheek braved rain, snow, freezing temperatures, dark of night and a spring during which sunshine and blooming times proved fiendishly elusive. Many individual sites were photographed at different times and seasons in his quest for the perfect image. His dedication to his art and to this project is evident on every page. Richard and I hope that our readers will come to share our enthusiasm and to understand our devotion to old Richmond today.

John G. Zehmer
Executive Director
Historic Richmond Foundation
May, 1988

St. John's Church, East Broad between 24th and 25th streets. William Byrd II, Richmond's founder, donated two lots on "Richmond Hill" for the construction of a simple frame building begun in 1739. Enlarged in 1772, it housed the Virginia Convention of 1775, where Patrick Henry made his famous denunciation of tyranny, ending with the immortal words "give me liberty or give me death." The interior of the transept, shown here, is the oldest part of the church. In its churchyard lie many early Richmonders including George Wythe, a signer of the Declaration of Independence who taught law to Thomas Jefferson, John Marshall and Henry Clay. As Richmond grew the name of the area was differentiated from that of the city and became "Church Hill."

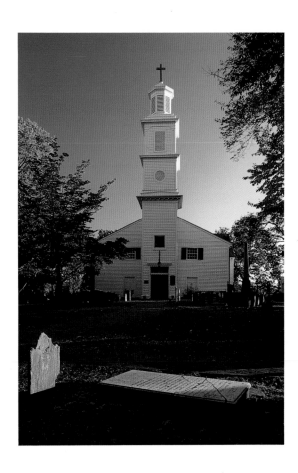

Elmira Shelton House, 2407 East Grace Street. The childhood sweetheart of Edgar Allan Poe, Elmira Shelton, was living here when they became engaged in 1849 just before his death. This typical Church Hill town house, across from St. John's Church, has been the headquarters of Historic Richmond Foundation (HRF) since the late 1950s. To ensure its survival, a unique wooden summerhouse was moved to the garden.

The Church Hill Pilot Block, 2300 Block East Grace Street. Church Hill includes Richmond's largest concentration of antebellum structures. The city established the St. John's Church Old and Historic District in 1957 to protect the neighborhood. The then newly formed Historic Richmond and others restored the houses in this block over a period of years, demonstrating the spectacular success achievable through public and private cooperation.

Above: **View Down the James River** from Church Hill. Just upriver from this curve are the Falls of the James River, a seven-mile stretch of rapids which mark the furthest inland point navigable by ocean-going ships. The flamboyant William Byrd II founded the town at the Falls in 1737 calling it "Richmond" because this view was reminiscent of the Thames seen from Richmond west of London.

Below: **St. John's Mews.** The Garden Club of Virginia landscaped the center of the Pilot Block as a community garden for Church Hill residents. To the existing stone alley were added a new summerhouse and important ornamental ironwork saved from buildings demolished in other parts of the city.

17th Street Market. For well over two centuries Richmonders have bought local vegetables, fish, game, and Christmas greenery here. The terracotta bull's head originally adorned the second city market located further west on Sixth Street and demolished long ago. A pair of bull's heads was incorporated in the 1986 structure, at least the fifth market building on this site.

Below: **Belle Bossieux Building,** 101-109 North 18th Street. This row of shops with residences above was built by Edmund Bossieux who named the block for his wife. He was from New Orleans which accounts for the galleried design. Its restoration was partially financed by HRF to serve as a catalyst for renovation in Shockoe Valley.

Edgar Allan Poe Museum, 1916 East Main Street. The small colonial structure is considered Richmond's oldest house and serves today as the nucleus of a museum for items relating to Richmond's most famous literary figure. Owned by the Association for the Preservation of Virginia Antiquities (APVA), the museum is operated by The Poe Foundation.

Masons' Hall, 1805 East Franklin Street. Opened in 1787 as an important social center in bustling Shockoe Valley, this hall is the nation's oldest Masonic lodge in continuous use. John Marshall and Edmund Randolph were among its members. It was used as a hospital during the War of 1812 and the Marquis de Lafayette, an honorary member, was entertained there in 1824 on one of his triumphant visits to the city.

Capitol Square. Thomas Jefferson designed the central section of the Capitol. Begun in 1785, it was the first full-scale temple-form building constructed since antiquity – a landmark of neoclassicism. The wings, added in 1906, contain the two houses of the Virginia General Assembly, the oldest continuously meeting representative assembly in the new world. Behind the Capitol rises the castle-like roof of Old City Hall. The tallest building is the current City Hall.

Washington Monument. Unveiled in 1858, the overall design and the equestrian statue were the work of noted American sculptor Thomas Crawford. Completed after Crawford's death by Randolph Rogers, the monument was featured on the great seal of the Confederacy and now serves as a logo for the City of Richmond.

Virginia State Capitol. In the Old Hall of the House of Delegates *(below)* John Marshall presided over the trial of Aaron Burr, the Virginia constitutional and secession conventions assembled, Robert E. Lee took command of Virginia's troops and the Confederate Congress met. In the Capitol's Rotunda *(opposite)* stands the only statue of George Washington sculpted from life. The General Assembly authorized Jefferson to commission the work from Jean-Antoine Houdon in 1785. Busts of the other seven Virginia-born presidents and Lafayette fill the niches.

Executive Mansion, Capitol Square. Virginia's governors live in the oldest continuously inhabited governor's mansion in the country, first occupied in 1813. The mansion's neoclassical design was by Boston's Alexander Parris. The front hall *(opposite)* leads to a ballroom, and the vista is closed through the last arch by the dining room, an addition of 1906.

Old City Hall, Broad between 10th and 11th streets. This Gothic fantasy, designed by Elijah Myers and constructed between 1887 and 1894, was a very real symbol of Richmond's resurgence after the Reconstruction era. The building was remarkable for its advanced technology in the use of concrete, glass brick, electricity and cast iron in the arches, columns and stairway of its interior courts. Old City Hall (*opposite above*) was the subject of two dramatic preservation battles. The first in the 1960s resulted in an exterior cleaning. The latter, spearheaded by Historic Richmond Foundation in the 1970s, led to its acquisition by the State and subsequent renovation by a private developer.

Below: **Morson's Row,** 219-223 Governor Street. These Italianate row houses are the only survivors of the elegant residences which once framed Capitol Square. Built in 1853, the row has now been renovated for state offices and forms a handsome backdrop to the Executive Mansion.

Monumental Church, 1224 East Broad Street. A fire at the Richmond Theatre on December 26, 1811, took the lives of over seventy people, including the governor. The next year a committee chaired by John Marshall commissioned a church to be built over the common grave of the victims. Robert Mills, America's first native-born professional architect, designed the domed, octagonal body of the structure as a church, and the dramatic portico *(opposite)* as a memorial. Symbols of mourning are found in the inverted torches on the marbleized columns, the abstract sarcophagi on the columns supporting the balcony and in the lacrimals (tear vials) on the portico's frieze. No longer a church, the structure is owned by HRF.

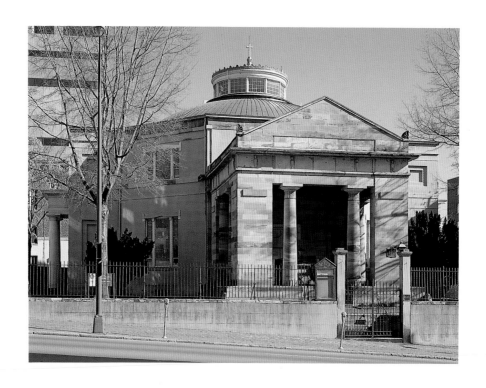

Previous pages: **Edward V. Valentine's Sculpture Studio,**
Valentine Museum, 1015 East Clay Street. In this studio Edward
Valentine sculpted his popular images of Southern heroes.
After his death the building was moved to the grounds of the
Valentine Museum, founded by his brother.

Opposite and below: **Wickham-Valentine House, Valentine Museum.** Designed by Alexander Parris, this elegant house was built in 1812 for John Wickham, an erudite lawyer and one of the city's wealthiest men. Its principal rooms feature neoclassical decorative paintings commissioned by Wickham and based on the designs of John Flaxman and Thomas Hope. In 1892 Mann Valentine II bequeathed the house, his varied collections and an endowment to establish a museum which now occupies the block.

Opposite and below: **John Marshall House,** 9th and Marshall streets. The great chief justice of the Supreme Court began this handsome house in 1788 and lived there for almost fifty years. He, his neighbor John Wickham and other lawyers gave the neighborhood its name, "Court End." An unusual plan and great number of Marshall possessions create a very special ambiance.

In 1907 the city acquired the house as a site for a new school. Demolition plans led to public outrage and it was left standing. In 1911 the city gave custodianship to the Association for the Preservation of Virginia Antiquities which has improved and maintained the property ever since.

White House of the Confederacy, 12th and Clay streets. Begun in 1818 the mansion has the typical Richmond arrangement with a small porch on the street and a large portico facing the rear garden. From 1861 to 1865 it served as the official residence of Confederate president Jefferson Davis and his family. Following twenty years as a school, the house was acquired in 1894 by the Confederate Memorial Literary Society and adapted for use as a museum. Now a part of the Museum of the Confederacy, the house has been restored to its Civil War appearance. The portrait of Davis by John Robertson (*opposite*) was painted in the house during the War.

Opposite above: **Egyptian Building,** 1223 East Marshall Street. In 1968 Virginia Commonwealth University (VCU) was formed from two existing institutions: the Medical College of Virginia (MCV) and the Richmond Professional Institute. The Egyptian Building, completed in 1846, originally housed the medical school and is one of the purest examples of its exotic architectural style. Even the cast iron fence is "Egyptian" with mummies for posts. From this single building MCV has grown to become a nationally recognized medical center.

Below: **Stephen Putney House,** 1012 East Marshall Street. Built in 1859, the house exhibits the most elaborate achievement of the Richmond iron industry. This and an adjacent house were slated for demolition by VCU, but were saved when its administration embraced historic preservation in the 1970s. Both now serve the Medical College as offices and meeting rooms.

Below: **First Baptist Church and First African Baptist Church,** Broad Street at 11th and at College streets, respectively. Black and white Baptists worshipped together until 1841 when the white members moved to a new building. The free blacks and slaves formed the First African Baptist Church which occupied the original building until the construction of a new one *(below left)* on the site in 1876. From the designs of Thomas U. Walter, the architect of the U.S. Capitol dome, the white Baptists built their new structure *(below right)* two blocks west. Both congregations eventually moved and their buildings were adapted for new uses by VCU.

Shockoe Slip, Cary and 13th streets. Since the 1970s the stores and warehouses in Shockoe Slip have been renovated for restaurants, entertainment and offices. Today its revitalized shops and apartments are part of a busy area that best symbolizes Richmond's successful combination of old and new.

Shockoe Slip Fountain. The heart of the Shockoe Slip Historic District is the triangular granite-paved "piazza." The fountain erected in memory of Charles S. Morgan, "one who loved animals," supplied water to the horses and oxen that once hauled goods through the area. Today it serves the horses of Richmond's beloved mounted police.

IN MEMORY OF
ONE WHO LOVED ANIMALS

Above: **The Great Shiplock and Tobacco Row,** Dock and Pear streets. The building of the James River Canal, championed by George Washington, was a major economic factor in Richmond's antebellum growth. Built to transfer goods around the falls, the canal eventually reached the Shenandoah Valley. The huge tobacco factories in the background are being renovated for new uses and constitute one of the largest preservation efforts in the country.

Below: **Tidewater Connection Locks,** 12th and Canal streets. Reynolds Metals Company designed parts of its plant to facilitate the restoration of sections of the canal. Water flows not only through the locks and under an arch of the old 13th Street bridge, but also under part of the factory itself.

Tredegar Ironworks, Tredegar Street *(left)* and the **Soldiers and Sailors Monument,** Libby Terrace and 29th Street *(right)*. High above the Great Shiplock at the east end of the canal, the figure atop the monument to the Confederate enlisted men looks west up the river and along the canal to the Tredegar Ironworks. The statue was the work of Richmond artist William Ludwell Sheppard. The cannon was cast by Tredegar, the chief supplier of munitions to the Confederacy. Portions of the factory have been restored by Ethyl Corporation and are included in the Richmond Canal Walk system.

Previous pages: **Roof of Main Street Station.** After a disastrous fire in 1983 destroyed its magnificent tile, the roof was meticulously reconstructed during the subsequent restoration of the gutted building.

Iron Fronts, 1000 Block East Main Street. Reminiscent of Venetian palaces, these ironfront buildings rose in 1866, literally from the ashes of the Evacuation Fire. Just over a century later they were renovated and continue as a part of Richmond's busy commercial district.

Exchange Place, 1309-1317 East Main Street. Unlike full iron fronts, these buildings have stucco or brick walls with cast-iron decorative trim. In spite of serious structural problems encountered during renovation, they were restored and opened in 1987.

Below left: **Main Street Station.** 16th and Main streets. Rising only a few feet from an elevated section of Interstate 95, the station's clock tower is a symbol of Richmond to millions of travelers. The chateau-like head house and enormous train shed, built in 1900, have been completely renovated.

Below right: **Planters National Bank Building,** 12th and Main streets. Even as the wrecking ball swung, protestors marched and a court injunction stayed the demolition crew. The happy result was the restoration and expansion of this 1893 Romanesque building which now houses the Virginia Supplemental Retirement System.

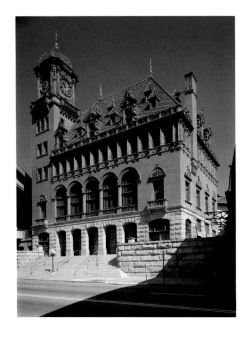

Previous pages: **Carpenter Center for the Performing Arts,** 600 East Grace Street. Completed in 1928 as part of the Loew's Theatre chain, this Moorish movie palace with its "atmospheric" auditorium was exquisitely restored and opened in 1983 as a theatre and concert hall. The original cloud machines still enliven the sky.

Left and above right: **St. Paul's Church,** 815 East Grace Street. Designed in 1845 by the Philadelphia architect Thomas Stewart, St. Paul's is the apogee of the Greek Revival in Richmond. Notable features are the intricate cast-iron fence, cast-iron Corinthian capitals, and the majestic plaster ceiling. It was in St. Paul's during the Sunday service on April 2, 1865, that Lee's courier handed Confederate President Davis the message that Richmond could no longer be defended and should be evacuated.

Below right: **St. Peter's Church,** 800 East Grace Street. Built in 1835 and the oldest Roman Catholic church building in Virginia, St. Peter's served as the cathedral of the Diocese of Richmond from 1841 until 1906. Many of the church's early members were German and Irish stonemasons who helped build the James River and Kanawha Canal.

Above and opposite: **Second Presbyterian Church,** 13 North 5th Street. Richmond's earliest Gothic Revival church is the only work in Virginia by noted Brooklyn architect Minard Lafever. The interior is dominated by the vast hammerbeam ceiling and the castellated pulpit and screen.

Below: **Stewart-Lee House,** 707 East Franklin Street. Used by Robert E. Lee's family during the Civil War, it was to this house that Lee returned, though only briefly, after the surrender. Owned by Historic Richmond Foundation, it has been adapted for commercial use.

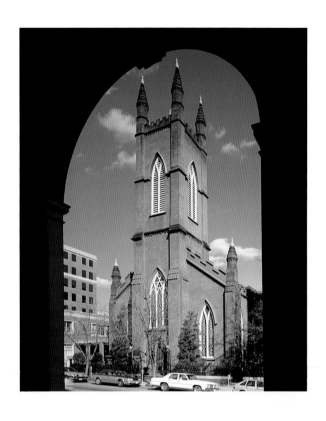

Barret House, 15 South 5th Street. One of a number of 1840s Greek Revival mansions built with stuccoed walls, stone trim and handsome ironwork, this is one of the best preserved. It was given by Mary Wingfield Scott, Richmond's pioneer preservationist, for use as the headquarters of the Virginia Society of the American Institute of Architects.

Ellen Glasgow House, 1 West Main Street. The home of the famous novelist for most of her life, the Greek Revival house and its neighbors figure prominently in Glasgow's works. The house was acquired by the APVA and was subsequently privately restored as a residence and offices.

Hancock-Wirt-Caskie House, 2 North 5th Street. This elegant dwelling, erected in 1808, is perhaps the best of an unusual group of Virginia houses which have half-octagons flanking central porches. For a brief period it was the home of William Wirt, author, politician and U.S. Attorney General. This and several nearby structures recall the fashionable residential neighborhood that once centered around 5th and Franklin streets.

Previous page: **200 Block West Franklin Street,** North Side. In 1977 Historic Richmond Foundation saved a total of eight houses, four on each side of the street, from demolition for high-rise development by finding sympathetic owners for each mansion.

Mayo-Carter House, 205 West Franklin Street. The Junior League of Richmond played a major role in the preservation of the 200 block of West Franklin Street by establishing its headquarters in this sophisticated 1895 mansion by Carrère and Hastings, the New York architects of the nearby Hotel Jefferson.

200 Block West Franklin Street, South Side. All of the major Richmond architectural styles of the 19th century are illustrated in the buildings of this and neighboring blocks. Renovation of these served as a catalyst for preserving similar ones nearby.

Kent-Valentine House, 12 East Franklin Street. Designed by Isaiah Rogers in 1844 and remodeled in 1910, this was the last of the downtown mansions to be privately occupied. It was restored in 1971 by The Garden Club of Virginia as its headquarters.

Linden Row, 100-114 East Franklin Street. The city's most impressive surviving row of houses was built in two phases in 1847 and 1853. Presented to Historic Richmond Foundation by Mary Wingfield Scott, the row is protected with restrictive covenants and has been refurbished for use as an inn.

Previous pages and below: **The Jefferson Sheraton Hotel,** 101 West Franklin Street. Major Lewis Ginter, Richmond benefactor and the tobacconist who packaged and promoted "cigarettes," believed Richmond should have a first-rate hotel and so built the magnificent Jefferson, opened in 1895. The hotel, including its Franklin Street façade seen here, was designed by Carrère and Hastings of New York. The original lobby with its monumental stair was rebuilt after a disastrous fire in 1901. In the early 1980s "The Jefferson," as it became affectionately known, was handsomely restored after years of neglect. The restoration of the stained-glass dome of the Palm Court was a major undertaking. Under it stands a statue of Jefferson by E.V. Valentine *(below)* flanked by pools which once held live alligators.

Bolling Haxall House, 211 East Franklin Street. The impressive Italianate mansion was built in 1858 by the owner of the Haxall Mills, one of the largest flour mills in the world at that time. Its Richmond-made iron fence, gate, balconies and window arches are exceptionally fine. In 1900 the house became the headquarters of The Woman's Club of Richmond – an early example of adaptive use.

Mayo Memorial Church House, 110 West Franklin Street. Built in 1841 and enlarged by tobacconist Peter Mayo in 1884, this house was given to the Episcopal Diocese of Virginia by Mayo's daughters in 1923. Its exuberant Victorian interiors, meticulously restored, make this one of Richmond's most unusual office spaces.

Science Museum of Virginia, 2500 West Broad Street. The inspiration for the former Broad Street Station was the Baths of Caracalla as modified in this monumental design by John Russell Pope, architect of the Jefferson Memorial and the National Gallery of Art. It has been sensitively adapted for use as the Science Museum of Virginia. The clock surrounded by the signs of the zodiac *(left)* is typical of the building's beautifully crafted classical details.

Previous pages: **Central Fidelity Bank,** 219 East Broad Street. The vaulted banking hall of the Art Deco skyscraper, for many years Richmond's tallest building, exhibits a dramatic interior equal to the prominence of its exterior. The bank was built to serve the Broad and Grace street merchants and is a landmark in the truest sense of the word.

Broad Street Historic District. Late nineteenth- and early twentieth-century commercial structures line Richmond's most prominent east-west street. The rows of stores and larger landmarks produce a kaleidoscope of architectural details ranging from Romanesque to Art Deco. Rehabilitation of the once-neglected façades began in earnest in the 1980s.

Empire Theatre, 118 West Broad Street. Originally a vaudeville house completed in 1910, the Empire is Richmond's oldest surviving theatre. Most of its delightful, almost whimsical, classical interior details survive. Restoration of the theatre was a pioneering preservation effort on Broad Street.

Maggie L. Walker House, 110½ East Leigh Street. As the centerpiece of Jackson Ward, the largest National Historic Landmark District associated with black history, the home of the courageous Mrs. Walker is now preserved by the National Park Service. Here the nation's first female bank president and the founder of the oldest existing black-owned bank in the nation reared her family and lived from 1904 until her death in 1934. In these rooms (left) she entertained and worked with many of the important civil rights leaders of her day.

Jackson Ward Historic District. One of the nation's greatest concentrations of architectural cast iron is to be found in this center-city neighborhood. It also features fine Greek Revival town houses, Queen Anne rows and a number of imposing public buildings like the First Battalion Virginia Volunteers Infantry Armory *(opposite above)* which housed Richmond's black regiment trained for service in the Spanish-American War. Jackson Ward's first residents included Richmond's early German and Jewish settlers. By the 1850s it had a significant free black population. From the 1880s to the present it has been the symbol of black culture, business and politics in the city.

Below: **Bill "Bojangles" Robinson,** Leigh and Adams streets. The world famous dancer was born a few blocks from the modern statue by John Temple Witt. The monument stands near the intersection where Robinson paid to have a traffic light installed for the safety of school children taking a route he used as a child.

Ebenezer Baptist Church, 216 West Leigh Street. One of the numerous churches located in Jackson Ward, this was an offspring of the First African Baptist Church. Ebenezer in its own right has been the mother of numerous other congregations. Ebenezer was instrumental in the founding of Hartshorn Memorial College which eventually became part of Virginia Union University.

Hebrew Cemetery, Hospital and 5th streets. Established in 1816, this burial ground features some of the best preserved headstones and iron work in the city. The fence surrounding the Confederate section with its draped rifles and crossed sabres is without peer.

Shockoe Cemetery and the Almshouse, Hospital Street. The cemetery contains the graves of many notables, including John Marshall, John Wickham, Peter Francisco and Elizabeth Van Lew, the illustrious Union spy whose grave is marked by a boulder sent from Boston by her "Massachusetts Friends." In the background is the Almshouse built in 1860 and used during the Civil War as a hospital and temporary home of the Virginia Military Institute. In the 1980s the building was rehabilitated as subsidized housing for the elderly.

WICKHAM

Previous pages: **Joseph Bryan Park.** After Joseph Bryan's death in 1908, his family donated approximately two hundred acres of land north of Ginter Park as a memorial. Bryan's civic, business and cultural efforts for the city were legion. By refusing a challenge and terming the practice of duelling "barbarous and absurd," he is credited with putting an end to duelling in Virginia. Today Bryan Park is well known for its thousands of azaleas.

Virginia Union University, North Lombardy Street and Brook Road. The product of several mergers of institutions in the 1890s, VUU traces its history back to the post-Civil War efforts of the Freedmen's Bureau to provide higher education for blacks. The University's buildings in the Romanesque style offer a lively contrast to the tower of the Belgian Building in the distance.

Because of the outbreak of World War II, Belgium gave its pavilion at the 1939 New York World's Fair to Virginia Union. It had been designed for re-erection in Belgium by Henri van de Velde, an important proponent of modern architecture. At the base of the tower are panels of sculpture *(below)* relating to Belgium and the Belgian Congo (Zaire).

Union Theological Seminary, 3401 Brook Road. This Presbyterian seminary was established at Hampden-Sydney College in 1812 and moved to Richmond in 1896. The quadrangle is enclosed by picturesque red brick Victorian buildings. The site was donated by Lewis Ginter as a focal point for his development of a new trolley suburb called "Ginter Park." As he envisioned, tree-lined residential streets now surround the seminary.

Bloemendaal, The Lewis Ginter Botanical Garden, 7000 Lakeside Avenue. This seventy-two-acre farm, bequeathed to the city by Grace Arents, Lewis Ginter's niece, is being transformed into a major horticultural center. Included in the plans is the adaptive use of Miss Arents' frame house and farm buildings.

Previous pages and opposite: **Monroe Park and Cathedral of the Sacred Heart.** Monroe Park serves as the eastern terminus of Virginia Commonwealth University's west campus and as a setting for a number of public buildings. The statue of General Williams Carter Wickham, C.S.A., by E.V. Valentine faces the Roman Catholic cathedral begun in 1903. The carefully preserved Renaissance detailing of the building is particularly fine.

Below: **The Fan District.** Monroe Park's pentagonal shape creates a street pattern resembling the sections of a fan – hence the area's popular name. Built up between the 1880s and the 1920s, the area contains over three thousand town houses in a variety of styles, many of which have been restored by enterprising home-owners. It is the largest designated historic district in Virginia.

The Mosque, Monroe Park. One of the city's most exotic structures, the Mosque's façade is reminiscent of a fortified Mogul palace. Built in 1926 as the Acca Temple Shrine, the Mosque was purchased by the city in 1940 and is still used for concerts and public meetings. The interior *(opposite)* is a potpourri of Indo-Moorish motifs.

92

Meadow Street Park. This is one of several triangular parks formed where the diagonal streets of "The Fan" cross the city's regular grid pattern. The park is dominated by a memorial to the famed First Virginia Regiment by Ferruccio Legnaioli.

VCU West Campus. Immediately west of Monroe Park in the "Lower Fan," Virginia Commonwealth University has undertaken the adaptive restoration of several whole blocks which include some of Richmond's most opulent late Victorian and Edwardian mansions. Perhaps the most significant is 901 West Franklin Street *(below)*, the robust Romanesque Revival home of Major Lewis Ginter, which also served as the city's first public library.

Temple Beth Ahabah, 1117 West Franklin Street. The interior of Beth Ahabah is dominated by a great dome on pendentives. Both the painting in the central arch and the organ are part of the original 1904 interior. The first Temple Beth Ahabah on 11th Street was dedicated in 1848 and replaced in 1880. The congregation moved to its spectacular Beaux Arts building (*above*) in 1904. Among its stained glass windows in the sanctuary is one by Louis Comfort Tiffany (*below*) depicting "Mount Sinai erupting at the very moment when God's presence became manifest to Moses."

Previous pages: **Branch House,** 2501 Monument Avenue. In 1916 John Kerr Branch, Jr., commissioned John Russell Pope to design this mansion both as a home and a setting for his art collection. The Tudor-style house has stately rooms with details from European houses. Carefully restored in the early 1980s it is now used for offices.

Below: **Monument Avenue.** In 1890 the noble statue of Robert E. Lee *(opposite)* by the French sculptor Jean Antonin Mercié was unveiled on the edge of a tobacco field at the end of Franklin Street. Soon the street was continued to the west and named "Monument Avenue." Over the next half century the grand boulevard developed with a total of five monuments, a wide median, four rows of trees and fine large houses. In 1980 the Lee Monument, owned by the Commonwealth, had its original dark patina restored.

Jefferson Davis Monument. Unveiled in 1907, its design by Richmond architect William C. Noland with sculpture by Edward Valentine is clearly that of a terminal feature. This was not to be, as additional monuments were added to the evolving avenue. The cannon in the foreground marks the site of a star fort, part of the inner ring of the Confederate defenses which protected Richmond on the west.

The Matthew Fontaine Maury Monument by Frederick William Sievers honors the inventor of the torpedo who was a Commander in the Confederate Navy. Sievers' design, however, emphasizes his subsequent contributions to oceanography for which he has been called "The Pathfinder of the Seas." It was unveiled in 1929.

2300 Block, Monument Avenue. The stately houses which line the avenue vary in style, size and material. The second, third and fourth houses from the right were designed respectively by Duncan Lee, William Lawrence Bottomley and the Baskervill firm. These architects are credited with many of the more important houses on the avenue. In the 1970s, citizens protested the city's plan to cover the original asphalt paving blocks with sheet asphalt. The ensuing "conversations" resulted in the designation by City Council of eleven blocks as a protected historic district. In this area the paving has been restored, handsome street lights installed and uniform tree planting accomplished. In the late 1980s, the four monuments owned by the city were cleaned and restored. The care and cooperation of the property owners and city government have assured the preservation of one of the most impressive urban spaces in the nation.

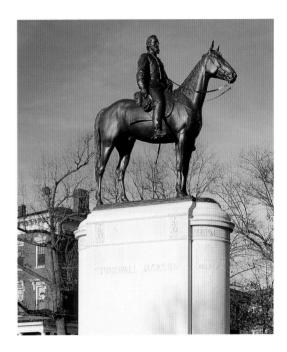

Above: **The T.J. "Stonewall" Jackson Monument,** by Richmond sculptor Frederick W. Sievers was unveiled in 1919. In 1907 the **J.E.B. Stuart Monument** *(below)* was unveiled in the same week as the Davis monument during a reunion of 18,000 Confederate veterans. It was the work of Fred Moynihan.

Previous pages, below and opposite: **Virginia House,** 4301 Sulgrave Road. In the 1920s, Ambassador Alexander Weddell and his wife purchased portions of Warwick Priory in England. From these they created Virginia House in a beautifully landscaped setting overlooking the James River in Windsor Farms, Richmond's frankly Anglophile suburb laid out in the 1920s. The rich interior woodwork is an appropriate setting for the Weddells' collection of *objets d'art* and architectural fragments. In 1948 the house and its gardens were bequeathed to the Virginia Historical Society. The property is used for meetings and social functions, as the Weddells intended.

Below and opposite. **Agecroft Hall,** 4305 Sulgrave Road. In the 1920s on land adjoining Virginia House, Mr. and Mrs. T.C. Williams, Jr., rebuilt Agecroft Hall, a fifteenth century English manor house seriously threatened by mining. Williams was one of the prime developers of Windsor Farms. Agecroft's leaded windows and intricate timberwork are especially notable. The house, now operated as a museum featuring Tudor and early Stuart furnishings, sits on a twenty-three-acre site embellished with flower gardens, an herb garden, an Elizabethan knot garden and romantic "English" views of the canal, the river and the countryside.

Wilton, South Wilton Road. Completed in 1753 by William Randolph III, this Georgian plantation house originally stood several miles down the James River in Henrico County. George Washington stayed the night at Wilton after Patrick Henry's "Liberty or Death" speech. The Marquis de Lafayette also enjoyed the Randolphs' hospitality near the end of the Revolution. To protect the house from encroaching industrialization, the National Society of Colonial Dames in America purchased Wilton in 1933 and had it dismantled and re-erected on another river site some fifteen miles away in Richmond's West End. Wilton exhibits some of the most beautiful paneling (*opposite*) in Virginia and furniture exemplary of the best American craftsmanship.

University of Richmond. Founded in 1832 as a Baptist seminary, the school was chartered eight years later as Richmond College. For many years the college was based in and around the Haxall mansion, Columbia. In 1914 the school moved several miles to the far West End and merged with the Baptist Woman's College to become the University of Richmond. The early buildings designed by Cram, Goodhue and Ferguson are outstanding examples of "Collegiate Gothic".

Byrd Theatre, 2908 West Cary Street. The domed interior of the Byrd Theatre, a lavishly decorated 1928 movie palace, is resplendent with murals, plaster work and a splendid chandelier that changes colors. Few theatre interiors have survived with so much intact. A mighty Wurlitzer organ still rises dramatically from the pit for concerts. In the late 1970s, the theatre was refurbished; fortunately, it has never needed restoration.

Previous pages and below: **Battle Abbey,** Boulevard at Kensington Avenue. In 1913, just as the Confederate Memorial Association was completing Battle Abbey, Thomas Fortune Ryan, the philanthropist responsible for the building of the Cathedral of the Sacred Heart, offered funds for a series of monumental murals. Charles Hoffbauer, the French artist chosen, began the series, but stopped to return home to fight in World War I. On his return from France, he revised the scheme to reflect the cruel realities of war he had so recently experienced. Since 1946, Battle Abbey has been the headquarters of the Virginia Historical Society, housing its library and galleries.

Hollywood Cemetery. One of the country's famous picturesque Victorian cemeteries is perched on rolling hills beside the James. Laid out in 1848 by John Notman, it was twelve years later the tragically obvious choice for a major Confederate cemetery. The dry stone pyramid of James River granite rises ninety feet above the ranks of 18,000 Confederate dead.

Hollywood Cemetery. The various monuments in Hollywood form a roster of famous and not so famous Richmonders. Neighbors in life often became neighbors in death. Here Jefferson Davis in bronze stands near statues marking the graves of his daughters. Other luminaries include John Tyler, George Pickett, J.E.B. Stuart, Matthew Fontaine Maury, Fitzhugh Lee, and authors Ellen Glasgow, James Branch Cabell and Douglas Southall Freeman.

Hollywood Cemetery. The unusual pavilion over the tomb of James Monroe is one of the finest examples of cast iron in the country. It was erected in 1859, a year after Monroe's remains were moved to Richmond from New York, twenty-eight years after the president's death. The iron dog *(below)* is an extraordinary ornament in a cemetery noted for its ironwork.

Previous pages, below and opposite: **Maymont.** The suburban estate of Major James H. Dooley and his wife, Sallie May, for whom Maymont was named, comprises a hundred acres of Belle Epoque fantasy overlooking the canal and the river. Gardens, grottoes and pavilions surround the 1890 stone mansion. Furniture and art collected by the Dooleys on their travels still fill the mansion and adorn the grounds. Mrs. Dooley, as requested by her husband, left the property to the city as a "museum and public park." The Maymont Foundation has restored the buildings and grounds and expanded public services since assuming management of the property in 1975. Maymont is famous for its children's programs, nature studies, carriage collection and historic interpretation.

William Byrd Park. The Carillon, Virginia's World War I memorial, sits in a lake-studded park named for the city's founder. City Council purchased 60 acres of land in the far western suburbs and began construction of a reservoir in 1874. Additional land was acquired for the large park over the next quarter century.

Above: View of downtown from the top of The Carillon.

Below: **The Pumphouse,** Byrd Park. Built in 1883 to force river water up to the Byrd Park reservoir, the Pumphouse was not only a utilitarian structure, but also a fantastic Gothic pavilion complete with a ballroom. The new trolley line, part of the first successful electric streetcar system in the world, brought the public from downtown to spend leisurely afternoons lolling by the river and exploring the course of the James River and Kanawha Canal.

The Falls of the James in the heart of Richmond.

Subjects

- Open to the public on a regular basis. Individual sites should be consulted for times and fees.
- Open by appointment.